# Bamboo Nation Constitution



**Transplant you're own country and watch it grow!**

ISBN: 1537265865
ISBN-13: 9781537265865

## Acknowledgments

For those brave souls of the past who dared stand up for their beliefs, declaring their independence, and drawing enough of a following to start something new and different, you have our respect.

## What is Bamboo Nation?:

Bamboo Nation is a proposed Proprietary Community that someday may become reality.

It represents an ideal balance between the fairness of a constitutional republic, the flexibility of a democracy, the defensive strength of a trained military force, and the freedom of individual liberty.

Tired of bureaucratic oppression and irresponsible authority figures that are exempt from the rules they enforce on everyone else?

Why not join, or start, a proprietary community where the people with authority must earn that authority and the people making the rules are part of the community?

## Preamble:

The symbol and theme of Bamboo Nation is bamboo. Bamboo is a plant that has long helped humanity. It is used as a building material which replenishes itself and expands year by year. The tender young shoots are a source of food, with some varieties being eaten raw and others requiring preparation through boiling, roasting, pickling, or other methods. The shavings, sap, waxy excretions, and for some varieties even the leaves have been used as medicine. The leaves and wood burn efficiently and hotter than many other plants, with less resin and creosote being produced. The charcoal produced from it is of high quality, often used in filtration of gases and liquids, with it's power of absorption being dependent on the temperature with which it was processed.

Though each pole and stalk of bamboo seems like an independent plant, and if separated with its own roots it can survive, the new plants are connected through their roots to their parents and siblings in a network of support that forms a larger organism.

There are two broad categories of bamboo, clumping types and running types. The clumping types flourish quickly and spread very slowly. The running types, once transplanted, put up new growth next to the parent plant during their first growth season.

After strengthening their roots, during their second growth season they put up new growth about 6 feet (~2 meters) away. During their third growing season, they have new growth about 12 feet (~4 meters) away from the initial site and they start filling in the center area with larger poles. Over the process of five growth seasons, it can sometimes fill an acre of land (over 43 thousand square feet or 4 thousand square meters).

These principles of usefulness and support combined with efficiency and independence represent the ideals of Bamboo Nation.

# Main Body:

## Article 1. System of Government:

The powers of government shall be divided into two groups. First is the Council of Citizens(Citizens Council) and second is the Guardians Troupe.

### I. Citizens Council powers and responsibilities:

a. The Citizens Council may organize community activities and projects.

b. They may propose rules and regulations that are not in violation of this constitution to the communities they represent, gather and tally the votes and suggestions, and record the decisions.

c. They may also repeal old rules and regulations by the same process.

d. All rules and regulations recorded by the Citizens Council will have an expiration date not to exceed twenty years from the date they are recorded.

e. If a specific expiration date is not set, those rules and regulations will automatically expire five years after they are recorded.

f. Within one year before regulations expire, the Citizens Council may propose to their community that a given rule or regulation be extended.

g. Council members may not be exempted from active rules or regulations.

h. In cases of dispute between individuals or groups, the Citizens Council may act as a court of decision.

i. Council members are encouraged to maintain regular employment in their communities.

## II. Citizens Council levels and members:

a. A Citizens Council may be formed for any community, small or large, even compound communities from national to local levels.

b. Members of a Citizens Council are representatives chosen by their communities, or their part of a given community, to coordinate the flow of information; organize activities and projects; and gather suggestions as well as votes.

c. A given council may appoint one member or individual to organize meetings, or this role may be delegated to a device or set procedure.

d. The position as a council member is not to be a paid or professional role, so as to encourage members to maintain their role as members of their communities. This does not preclude communities from supporting them in their duties by providing temporary lodging, meals, or transportation.

## III. Guardians Troupe powers and responsibilities:

a. Members of the Guardians Troupe, "Guardians", shall make themselves available in times of emergency to assist in restoring safety and security, and in some cases to carry out justice.

b. In the case of violent invasion by a foreign power or subversive group, the Guardians may be called on for national or community defense.

c. The Guardians may exercise great discretion in carrying out their duties, however the use of excessive or lethal force is not to be authorized.

d. It is understood that in emergency and defense situations, property damage; injuries; and even deaths may result. Guardians involved in such encounters will undergo evaluation and if necessary mental reconditioning and physical retraining, so that they may better serve their communities.

e. Mental reconditioning may be as simple as counseling for post traumatic stress or as involved as hypnotherapy to treat deep rooted mental illnesses.

e. Guardians may assist and advise their communities in various projects in various capacities.

f. Guardians are encouraged to engage in secondary occupations so as to be of greater assistance to their communities and to be close by when their assistance is needed.

## IV. Guardian Troupe Levels and members:

a. The Guardian Troupe is to be a hierarchical organization with national and local chapters.

b. Entry into and position in the Guardian Troupe is based on tests of one's knowledge and skill levels.

c. Training in these skills may be offered to the general public.

d. Skills required at different levels include:

Apprentice: Non-lethal self defense fundamentals

Break-falls, rolls, and jumping.

Meditation for emotional control and conflict preparation.

Basic postures, forms, & techniques.
Forms/techniques for larger opponents.
Forms/techniques for faster/knife-wielding opponents.
Forms/techniques for opponents with a sword/long-reaching weapon.

Defender/Scout: Protection/Counter terrorism methods & martial arts core skills

Making training equipment.

Strengthening & toughening the body.
Running/fighting postures.
Mental attitude.
Quick counters to common techniques.
Weapon disarming techniques.
Surprise attacks.
Dealing with surprise attacks.
Conflict disrupting techniques.

Squad Leader/Captain: Tactical Training

In depth striking & grappling principles.

Pressure points.
Countering combos.
Military moral code, conflict/damage minimizing principles, and broad perspective.
Weapons: Staves, pikes, spears, halberds/pole-arms, swords, throwing knives, Zen archery

Survival skills: Fire-making, building shelters & barricades, finding food & water
Moving in groups & formations
Strategy: Making use of terrain, weather, & timing.

General: Specialized Training for Extreme situations

Training in nature for strength.

Close quarters combat from standing & sitting.
Dealing multiple opponents.
Rope binding methods.
Meditation for calm focus in extreme situations.

Negotiator: Basic psychology & interrogation methods, specialized training for capturing violent individuals

Philosophy of gentle flexibility.

Techniques for arresting/immobilizing opponents.
Techniques for multiple opponents at the same time.
Using trunction tools for trapping blades and jamming guns.
Using short wide blades for deflecting projectiles and disarming opponents.
Using rifles for non-lethal precision shooting.
Using pistols for quick-draws and trick shots.
Bare handed blade catching.

Special Operations: Specialized Training for Delicate situations

Humble moral code, conflict/damage avoidance principles, and broad perspective.

Use of blunt, bladed, and flexible tools.
Use of specialized tools.
Body conditioning and skills for healing/recovering from injuries.
Extreme climbing and jumping skills.
Basic techniques for manipulating opponents.
Specialized walking and running techniques.

Operations Coordinator: Specialized Training for Communications/intelligence and Counter-espionage

Escape strategies.

Weather predicting.
Manufacturing using local resources.
Biology & medicine.
Psychology including animal behavior.
Stealth and infiltration techniques.
Transportation and communication technology.

Regional Leadership: All of the above in addition to:

Advanced esoteric techniques.

World religions and philosophies.

## Article 2. Standardized Currency:

The basic unit of currency to be issued by the Bamboo Nation for domestic transactions, which may be referred to as the Water Dollar such other names are deemed appropriate, shall be standardized to the value of one liter (~one quart) of distillation purified water. Water is a substance essential to the life of organic (carbon based) lifeforms.

Plants use water, along with carbon dioxide from the air and trace substances from the soil, to produce food and other important substances. Humans and other creatures use food and water to produce the energy we need to live and to perform activities. As such this fundamental currency of life, so necessary for many working processes, becomes the currency of commerce as well, purchasing the goods and services that wouldn't exist without it.. This Water Dollar currency may be issued in whatever denominations are deemed convenient.

## Article 3. Sources of Revenue:

### I. Option to tax and limits thereupon:

a. For the sake of funding projects organized at the national or community level, with the approval of the citizens, a tax may be levied on sales of goods and services.

b. Said tax, whether levied at the national or the community level shall not exceed 5% of the sale price. For compound communities, the total compound tax (local community tax + larger community tax + national tax) on a given transaction must not exceed 15% of the total sale price.

c. There shall be no taxes levied directly against an individuals income or property.

### II. Alternative sources of revenue:

a. The national and/or local Citizens Council may elect to sell one or more products to citizens and foreigners.

b. The national and/or local Citizens Council may provide utilities for a fee.

c. For water as a utility service or as a product, distilled water shall be billed at a rate of one water dollar per liter. Mechanically filtered and chemically purified water shall be billed at a lower rate. (This does not preclude private companies from charging their own rates for packaging or the supposed benefits of source dependent mineral inclusions)

d. National and local Guardian Troupes may provide special services and take on extra jobs for a fee.

## Article 4. Freedom of Speech & Right of Silence:

People have the ability to speak, to read & write. Provided they are prepared to deal with the consequences of sharing information (i.e. people's emotional reactions to what is being expressed), one may communicate whatever one wishes; in whatever form one is able to; to whoever is able to understand it. By the same token, one may choose to withhold said information regardless of attempts at persuasion.

## Article 5. Freedom of Religion:

The ability to choose how one interprets things and what one believes is fundamental to humanity. As such the government shall not presume to dictate to people as to matters of faith. So long as they don't violate any laws, or anyone else's rights, people may practice their religion as they see fit.

## Article 6. Freedom of Privacy & Right of Observance:

Privacy, the quality or state of being apart from undesired company or observation; or freedom from unauthorized intrusion, is a privilege granted by technology [in the form of walls or clothes] and by the polite manners of the people around us. It would be inappropriate for said privilege to be ignored outside of a justifiable emergency. Conversely, the ability to perceive the world and occurrences in the environment is fundamental to all life. Those who allow themselves and their conversations to be observed have no cause to censure the rights of others to observe their surroundings.

## Article 7. The Right to Life & the Right to Choose:

From the time one is born, or capable of living as an organism separate from one's parents, one has the right to live as long as one is able. One also has the right to do as they wish to the body they were born with, even if that choice leads to ending one's life. The government presumes no right to force one to live longer than one is willing or able to do.

## Article 8. Age of Consent:

a. From the age of twenty(20) one's body is considered to fully or sufficiently developed that no age related restrictions may be imposed.

b. From the age of eighteen(18) one is considered to be of sound enough mind to enter contracts without the approval of a parent/guardian.

c. From the age of sixteen(16) one is considered to be of sound enough mind to enter contracts with the approval of a parent/guardian.

d. From the age of thirteen(13) one is considered to be maturing sexually and emotionally capable of giving consent. Nonetheless, if that consent is found to have been obtained through coercion, especially by an authority figure, it will be considered inappropriate.

e. From the age of ten(10) one is considered to be of sufficient awareness to make decisions as to where and with whom they wish to live.

f. From the age of five(5) one's personality is considered to be fully formed, allowing one to pursue a course of education and learning.

g. If evidence can be provided relating to one's maturity; competence; and necessity, these may be adjusted for individual circumstances by the decision of the Citizen's Council.

## Article 9. Borrowing and Credit:

Neither the Citizens Council, nor the Guardians Troupe may borrow money using the credit of Bamboo Nation. They may upon request, issue a line of credit to other nations.

## Article 10. Citizenship, Naturalization, and Suffrage:

To become naturalized as a citizen of Bamboo Nation, one must be able to pass a test on the constitution and the laws; rules; and regulations of Bamboo Nation, and sign an affidavit stating that intends to follow all of those. This same test will be required of all citizens before they vote or take part in the Citizens Council. A fee may be charged for processing and recording the results of the tests as well as the affidavits. Those who pass may be given a Bamboo Nation passport.

## Article 11. Penalties:

Those who are not in accord with the constitution, laws, rules, and regulations of Bamboo Nation will be subjected to an evaluation of their situation by the Guardians, who may present their case to the Citizens Council for trial. Depending upon the severity of the situation, they may be reprimanded and reminded of the rule/regulation; relocated to a different area or community; required to undergo a course of psychological reconditioning under the supervision of a qualified member of the Guardian Troupe; some combination thereof; or in the worst cases exiled and banned from the Bamboo Nation with no citizenship status.

## Article 12. Admission and Formation of Communities:

a. Communities with 500 or more people, who ratify the Bamboo Nation constitution with a majority vote by two thirds(2/3) of the voting population, and form a Citizens Council, and set up a meeting hall/training area for the Guardian Troupe may be admitted to the Bamboo Nation regardless of their physical location.

b. Communities of 100 or more people may officially form within land or territory controlled by Bamboo Nation by forming a Citizens Council.

## Article 13. Freedom of Assembly:

The people may gather for any peaceful purpose, whether personal; cultural; or business. It is recommended that they post in advance advertising the nature of the gathering and the procedure for participating. If they are to assemble on lands maintained by the government, it is recommended that they organize said meeting through the Citizens Council.

## Article 14. The Right to Liberty:

Save for extraordinary circumstances, everyone is born free. Any attempts at enslavement and captivity must be imposed by an outside party. With the exception of a program of mental reconditioning, one may not be deprived of their basic liberties except by their own temporary or contractual agreement or lack of insistence to the contrary.

## Article 15. The Right to Pursue Happiness and Freedom of Enterprise:

It is the nature of all lifeforms to pursue their own happiness and satisfaction. It is not possible for an outside force to stop this pursuit. Toward this end, one may engage in any business or enterprise which does not interfere with the rights of others, nor violate the rules and laws of the land.

## Article 16. Limitations of Liability:

If a consumer is provided with a defective product they may reasonably request and be awarded a replacement or refund, especially if they can show or explain the defect. One who has been injured though the fault of another may reasonably request the other party to pay or do restitution up to the point that their injury has been healed or circumnavigated. If the restitution is financial, the amount shall not be greater than double the amount necessary for appropriate medical treatments.

## Article 17. Multiple Nationalities:

Citizens of Bamboo Nation may hold citizenship status in any number of other countries or nations.

## Article 18. Bearing Arms and Other Tools:

Arms or armaments are tools that can be used as weapons for attack or defense. There is no tool, device, or garment that cannot be employed as such by skilled or desperate persons. As such, there shall be no restrictions on the ownership of any given tool that an individual might find useful in their livelihood, or that might be used to defend themselves or others.

## Article 19. On Personal Ownership and the Right of Possession:

Except for inheritance and prenatal gifts, each person is born owning only their own mind and body. From that point on, through the kindness of others; and one's own efforts and skills, one may come into possession of many things. They are yours to hold; give; or sell, as long as you cultivate; preserve; maintain; and protect them. If they are abandoned; abused; and neglected, they may be taken up; cared for; and claimed by another.

## Article 20. On the Right to Unionize and the Protection of Competition:

It is natural that during hard times certain sectors of the economy may choose to join together to increase their bargaining power as a union or guild. These may be producers, manufacturers, merchants, employers, laborers, or some other group. Even after a situation has resolved, these groups tend to maintain their existence rather than give up their position and sometimes become nearly monopolies that dominate the field and harm or eliminate competition. The remedy for this is for a Citizen's Council to locally recognize said group as an incorporated entity with it's members, whether individuals or businesses, as employees or representatives of that singular entity once they have dominance over half or more of a market.

The best protection for a consumer is to know who they are dealing with and the best motivation for professionals and companies to do well by their customers is to maintain a good reputation. Toward that end, the Citizen's Counsel may collect consumer reports as well as the claims and statements made by businesses and professionals and make these publicly accessible. The best way for individuals to maintain their health and make appropriate decisions is to be well informed. As such the Citizen's Counsel may compile information from various scientific and cultural sources on the nutritional values and medicinal effects of various foods; substances; and products, as well as the effects of various exercises; therapies; and treatments, and make said information publicly available. Of course medical and health care professionals and companies will be included in the aforementioned consumer reports.

## Signatures:

Name: Contact information:

1.
2.
3.
4.
5.
6.
7.
8.
9.
10.
11.
12.
13.
14.
15.
16.
17.

18.

19.

20.

21.

22.

23.

24.

25.

26.

27.

28.

29.

30.

31.

32.

33.

34.

35.

36.

37.

38.

39.

40.

41.

42.

43.

44.

45.

46.

47.

48.

49.

50.

51.

52.

53.

54.

55.

56.

57.

58.
59.
60.
61.
62.
63.
64.
65.
66.
67.
68.
69.
70.
71.
72.
73.
74.
75.
76.
77.

78.

79.

80.

81.

82.

83.

84.

85.

86.

87.

88.

89.

90.

91.

92.

93.

94.

95.

96.

97.

98.
99.
100.

101.
102.
103.
104.
105.
106.
107.
108.
109.
110.
111.
112.
113.
114.
115.
116.

117.

118.

119.

120.

121.

122.

123.

124.

125.

126.

127.

128.

129.

130.

131.

132.

133.

134.

135.

136.

137.

138.

139.

140.

141.

142.

143.

144.

145.

146.

147.

148.

149.

150.

151.

152.

153.

154.

155.

156.

157.

158.

159.

160.

161.

162.

163.

164.

165.

166.

167.

168.

169.

170.

171.

172.

173.

174.

175.

176.

177.
178.
179.
180.
181.
182.
183.
184.
185.
186.
187.
188.
189.
190.
191.
192.
193.
194.
195.
196.

197.

198.

199.

200.

201.

202.

203.

204.

205.

206.

207.

208.

209.

210.

211.

212.

213.

214.

215.

216.

217.
218.
219.
220.
221.
222.
223.
224.
225.
226.
227.
228.
229.
230.
231.
232.
233.
234.
235.
236.

237.

238.

239.

240.

241.

242.

243.

244.

245.

246.

247.

248.

249.

250.

251.

252.

253.

254.

255.

256.

257.
258.
259.
260.
261.
262.
263.
264.
265.
266.
267.
268.
269.
270.
271.
272.
273.
274.
275.
276.

277.

278.

279.

280.

281.

282.

283.

284.

284.

286.

287.

288.

289.

290.

291.

292.

293.

294.

295.

296.

297.
298.
299.
300.
301.
302.
303.
304.
305.
306.
307.
308.
309.
310.
311.
312.
313.
314.
315.
316.

317.

318.

319.

320.

321.

322.

323.

324.

325.

326.

327.

328.

329.

330.

331.

332.

333.

334.

335.

336.

337.
338.
339.
340.
341.
342.
343.
344.
345.
346.
347.
348.
349.
350.
351.
352.
353.
354.
355.
356.

357.

358.

359.

360.

361.

362.

363.

364.

365.

366.

367.

368.

369.

370.

371.

372.

373.

374.

375.

376.

377.

378.

379.

400.

401.

402.

403.

404.

405.

406.

407.

408.

409.

410.

411.

412.

413.

414.

415.

416.

417.

418.

419.

420.

421.

422.

423.

424.

425.

426.

427.

428.

429.

430.

431.

432.

433.

434.

435.

436.

437.

438.

439.

440.

441.

442.

443.

444.

445.

446.

447.

448.

449.

450.

451.

452.

453.

454.

455.

456.

457.
458.
459.
460.
461.
462.
463.
464.
465.
466.
467.
468.
469.
470.
480.
481.
482.
483.
484.
485.

486.
487.
488.
489.
490.
491.
492.
493.
494.
495.
496.
497.
498.
500.

## How to get started:

1. Talk to your family, friends, and coworkers. Have them read this book and sign it if they agree that this is the kind of rules they want to live under.
2. Start training! Without skilled Guardians to protect and serve your new nation, it won't survive. It's your country, so get involved, build your skills, and invite friends to join you!
3. Buy or lease land to resell or rent out and make following the Bamboo Nation Constitution part of the property agreements. You can also setup Municipal Utility Districts and Home Owners Associations, or convince the members of existing associations and districts.
4. Help people, training those who are willing to learn, and help more people.
5. Protect, maintain, and expand your country slowly. Develop logos and signs to sell the idea to visitors/tourists.

That's it! Don't declare your independence until you have the resources to survive, and absolutely must.

https://www.facebook.com/BambooNation/

www.ingramcontent.com/pod-product-compliance
Lightning Source LLC
Chambersburg PA
CBHW070129290526
45789CB00005B/2178
*9781537265865*